CONTENTS

Title Page	1
Copyright	2
Dedication	3
Another Day	11
Photographic Memory	12
All we have in this world	13
A Journey Travelled	14
Brave	16
Filling in Time	17
A time so Far Away	18
Driftwood	20
Winter Rain	21
Forever	22
My First Day	24
Tangled	25
Promised Ghost	27
Dark Mirror	28
Lifeboat	29
Different Tracks	30
Weighted Smoke	32
Tobacco Scent	33

POETRY IS..GRIEF AND LOSS

Whispers From the Void

AJ Harvey

Copyright © 2020 AJ Harvey

All rights reserved

The characters and events portrayed in this book are fictitious. Any similarity to real persons, living or dead, is coincidental and not intended by the author.

No part of this book may be reproduced, or stored in a retrieval system, or transmitted in any form or by any means, electronic, mechanical, photocopying, recording, or otherwise, without express written permission of the publisher.

ISBN-13: 9781234567890
ISBN-10: 1477123456

Cover design by: Art Painter
Library of Congress Control Number: 2018675309
Printed in the United States of America

I dedicate this book to my Husband Ian for all his support and encouragement in the making of this book. Love you Hubby!

Us	34
Frosted Memory	36
Clown	38
Salt Blind	39
Sorrow is a Psychopath	40
Candlewax	42
The Timeglass	43
Starstruck	45
Summer Frost	46
No More Love Songs	47
On the Other Side	48
Wrecked	49
Eyes Closed	50
Hello	51
All I See	53
Walking the Wire	55
Endings	57
Life Again	58
Lifetime	60
Feather Flight	61
Days of Summer	62
Remember	64
Dust	65
I thought I Saw	66
Best	70
Western Wind	72
Telling tales	73
Afterword	75

About The Author 77

ANOTHER DAY

When you reside in a world of perpetual sorrow

The heart is unable to decide

Whether to laugh or cry

But the sun will always rise on the morrow

Bringing warm light to another day

So maybe there is room for both

PHOTOGRAPHIC MEMORY

A photographic view on day
Smiles held frozen, forever
No worries and cares yet to show
On these faces that shine
Lit with abandoned joy
Smiling into a blue framed sun
Eyes closed, I can smell the salt
Of a lapping tide
Feel the sand between my toes
Warmed by summer play
Time has long passed
Childhood has gone to rest
I mourn the loss
As the golden sun sets

ALL WE HAVE IN THIS WORLD

All we have in this world

Is time

To find our hopes and dreams

A blink and it goes

Like a comet

Your life, a scorching trail

Burning the days that you leave behind

On this planet of your birth

You lived

A life of wondrous adventure

You loved, were loved

A family tree planted

Nurtured and cherished

Look how the branches spread

A JOURNEY TRAVELLED

Lay down your head

On soft velvet clover

Breath in the perfume bed

As cotton white clouds drift over

Slowly walls break stone by stone

As the silence hits, hard as a hammer

Are you lonely? You are alone

Amidst the wreckage, as memories stir

A journey travelled by crooked road

Each turn a choice, or was it a destiny woven

Every step taken carries a load

And the weight grows with each path chosen

Regrets? There were a few rocks in the road

Second chances are like fairy powder

You don't get chance to reload

A life lived, is a life, so live it louder

BRAVE

Terrible times call for

Bravery

But to be brave

You don't need to face terrible times

You just

Need to open your eyes on another day

FILLING IN TIME

I am just filling time
Sleeping through dark times of the day
As dreams compete with the daily mind grime

Following the human way
Eating my fill of the ritual, survival routine
Facing life in the best possible way

Loving, hating, crying when I can, Guess I'm
Following the birth to death plan
Just by filling in time

A TIME SO FAR AWAY

A Long ago, in a time that seems so far away
Doesn't that sound so much like a cliché?
A time before grown up became a word
When a day lasted forever, isn't that absurd?
Wishes you made on a shooting star came true
Really? What other lies were told to you?
A four-leaf clover brings good luck,
There is gold at rainbows end. But, all you find is muck.

A time so far away was my childhood
I wish I had known, wish I had understood
That a day is not forever, they pass in a blink
Each day creating another memory in the chain link.
I am grown now and I have seen the shooting star.
I haven't made a wish on this fiery rock from afar
It wouldn't hear me as it travels the sky
Heading to earth on its final death cry.

It has filled the news these last few weeks
Nothing to be done, no deterrents to seek.
The world leaders have head for cover

Hoping they will be able survive once it's over.
People look to each of their religions
Hoping for some divine interventions.
They scream and rage against what is to be
Fighting in the streets in their fearful agony.

Two days to go and I have a spot picked.
I have a list, all boxes ticked.
Music, wine and a blanket to rest
For my faithful doggy companion on this quest
In the forest of my childhood play
I will find the mossy bed where I will finally lay.
To smell the earth and hear the birds last song.
Knowing all to soon it will be forever gone.

DRIFTWOOD

Cast adrift on a molten sea
Lost is the anchor, the tether
That held me, safe and secure
I am driftwood
With no course, no destination
Lost amongst the salted foam
I am carried to a distant horizon
Where a sun kissed sky, bleeds into the sea

Where is my safe harbour?
He is gone. Left for another shore
A whirlpool, I was spun around
Pulled into him, drowning.
Then cast out, abandoned.
I am driftwood
floating on fast, warm currents
I will go where they carry me
Until I hear the call of a new shore

WINTER RAIN

Words form on the tongue,

But they fall from your lips unspoken

Like winter rain

They crystalize pain

 My burning heart feels the chill, it's done

A tear says farewell to a love turned frozen

FOREVER

Like wine, intoxicating
I am an addict.
The look of you
The smell of you
My heat burns against your ice
There is no thaw.
I give all to you
My very soul to you
But I am distant in your eyes
A tracing paper image
Unknown to you
Not known to you
It is a lie, deceit bruises your lips
As they tumble in haste
I am torn from you
Restrained from you
In torturous fire I watch
As you walk away with her
She is nothing to you
She is nothing

Tomorrow, you will see

I will show her fickle heart

Then you and I, we will be

Forever

MY FIRST DAY

Counting steps, watching you fly
I can't catch your wind
It's gone in a deep billowing sigh
Seeing your wide smile, but I am thick skinned
So, your scattering insults will bounce away
Into the dark halo around you
Did I really want you to stay?
Go, leave these happy days, so very few
I won't be sad, no tears will wet my cheek
I can breathe deep again, I can take a breath
I can become the strong, leave the meek
Rise up from this suffocating death
So, fly away, find another path, Leave
Without a glance behind, I won't be there
Waving in sorrow, I will not grieve
For suddenly my dancing has flare
And I can laugh out loud, sing off key
Find friends that you pushed away
For they saw, what I now can see
Me. Without you. This is my first day.

TANGLED

Kisses trace my lips like paper
They are distant in their touch
And your smile, barely shows
On your face, it says so much

Your words in their normal flow
Say you are here, but I feel you go
Eyes already looking to see the third angle
In this emotional warring tangle

Does she feel the same pull of me?
As you leave her, does she see
How the tug of war plays out
When you say I love you, is it to her, or me

I saw her today in the park
Her toddler in her arms, his hair was dark,
And his eyes were your colour, warm brown
I sank into tears so deep, I could drown

I should cut the cord, let you go
But you have been so long part of my heart flow
It's no easy break, No easy cut

But, I know you love her. Isn't there always a but!

So, a choice is what now faces me
Sharing the heart, you don't share exclusively
Or let you go, be the father and husband
Your eyes tell me, the choice is already planned.

PROMISED GHOST

You told me you loved me
But it was lost in a day
Time was given, but I see
The world turned the sun away
I was holding onto a promised ghost
My fingers slipped into the mist
Nothing to hold onto, we almost,
Almost believed it when we kissed
But the poison grew and grew
I saw your battle turn into war
Your eyes gritted pain, looking for rescue
Then, and then, you were no more
Lost in a day
We were given time, but I see
The sun has turned away
Now I don't have you, loving me

DARK MIRROR

Reflections crystalize into blackened ice

As my laughter falls like pebbled hail

Cracking the dark mirror

My face falls into the deep black

My voice follows

Fading

To silence

Light bounces upon sunken hope

The pull is an anchor to the surface

Coloured blue in crystal glass

I inhale the warming hue

My heart stutters

Breaking

Through black

LIFEBOAT

Looking for the lifeboat

That is hidden amongst this life's wreckage sway

Broken pieces of the heart, that fell from you, from me

Did we always have this hate, hidden away?

Now cracked open for all to see

Because loving you, changed into loving me

Want to be on a different path, live a different way

I want to find who I used to be, breakaway from us, from we

My love, there is no lifeboat

The poison is hidden too deep, accrued from our yesterday

A goodbye is our only release now, it's meant to be

Don't say another word, It's our final day

Let's leave with our shared true love memory

DIFFERENT TRACKS

Eyes open onto a damp Tuesday
One dismal day out of the seven
Where clouds heavy with rain, stay
Blocking the promise of a summer heaven

I can smell the static of a brewing flash
And a false calm brings a hush to natures chatter
A boom breaks the silence, lit by a lightning clash
Storms in summer are worse, but does it matter?

Joy of chasing the rain in puddle splashes
Was a childhood game, and I still recall
Bright lightning sizzles and thunder bashes
As our laughter challenged the electric fireball

Heroic and rash, we ran with the changing wind
Years and years of foolish choices
Grown from our parents disciplined
Hand, we began to speak with our own voices

But storms can twist lives and how they change
Pulled apart onto different tracks
I saw you fall into a world dark and strange

You lived with strangers, zombie insomniacs

Laughter left your eyes, leaving them dark and hollow
I tried, I did, to show you that there was another way
But where the pack leads, you follow
You didn't see me, had nothing to say

But like the storm, I always will look for the spark
That lightning bolt, that will bring you the strike
Of reality, so you can see a way out from the dark
And I will be here to help you back into the light

WEIGHTED SMOKE

How heavy do we stroll across the world?

Solid stone, are our footsteps

As we breathe, our heartbeats counting down

Until, we float away like weighted smoke

And our footprints are all that remain

TOBACCO SCENT

How I yearn for the old days
Grieving the loss of tobacco scent
My grandad carried around
Clinging to crisp ironed shirts
Standing like a giant, his eyes twinkling blue
Holding memories of a time before

How his laughter comes quick to mind
Infectious as a rash
And I miss the feel of his hand in mine
As we walked down familiar streets
His pace unhurried and sure
Feeling safe and warm

US

Used to be tangled with you
Stuck together like superglue
It was we, us, one half of two
Mind reading, amazing but true
Yeah, you knew my brain too
But isn't that what couples do?

It was like when Juliette found her mate
Star-crossed lovers, it felt like fate
I remember our very first date
The apologies, when you arrived late
The film we saw, the popcorn we ate
The goodnight kiss, making my heart accelerate

Six months later, under a neon moon
A diamond needed an answer, and soon
After, in the rose scented month of June
Vows were made as bride and groom
How tender the night of our honeymoon
As our hearts sang in perfect tune

A lifetime of you and me
Now it's just me, I no longer see

You in the rooms where you used to be
A ghost in the misted dreams of memory
But I can still visit the place where I, becomes we
Just need to open the door with the love-heart key

FROSTED MEMORY

Cracked splinters
Fracture a perfect thought
Of you
And I see you in the reflections
Of a frosted memory

I don't
Want to freeze in the heat
Of the last words spoken
You are
Gone into history
And the void filters through
Me

Every silver lining is tied to a cloud
Dark and full of rain
There can be light
But you have to go through the pain

You smile but it's only a frown
That's been turned on its head
A mask of what you have to hide
Showing the joy, when you're crying instead

Ambushed by friends' good feelings
You can drown in their commiserations

Pity me. I am lost in the dark,
Dark day. Only the night shows a starry light
There I can let my mind float into the void
Hitch a ride on a searing comet flight

Grief is absent in the hours of the day
Hidden under a 'I'm doing well', look
But at night I can hug it close, like a blanket
Breathe in the sorrow like a well-read book

Sadness is a jigsaw picture I can't complete
When you are the missing piece of the puzzle

CLOWN

I am just the painted clown
Features hidden under greased concrete
Can you see the cracks as I smile?
A colourful costume covers the scars
Nothing to see here.

Running around in circles
Falling into deep water to applause of strangers
I can hear the laughter as I drown in buckets of stardust
Another pie in the face
Can't feel the pain.

There is one who knows my true name
They have seen my true face
Love carried us flying on the high trapeze
But when you fell, no net to catch the fall
Grief now wears a red nose.

SALT BLIND

Pale tears fill a salted sea

You are lost from me

Grief scattered in rock filled pools

Lit by sunlight shards

They glitter and spark

I am blinded

My sight of you lost to me

As tears salt a pale rising sea

SORROW IS A PSYCHOPATH

I am not the psychopath
That you colour
In the pages of your life
I see the aftermath
Of the words that slur
As you throw the blame and strife

I am not the psychopath
You see in glasses tinted black
I am only the one who can see
All the pain hidden in the wrath
I am not hiding my comfort in an attack
Put aside the hurt and the angry

Remember a time before the tears
When love held us in tight embrace
Before the loss tore us apart
Blinded we have hidden behind the fears
But love still lingers, a trace
It rests amongst your grief-stricken heart

See the world, it continues to turn
Bringing a new sun, a new moon
See me in the darkened cloud
Take my hand, it won't burn
Melt into my protective cocoon
A sorrow shared, shuts out the crowd

CANDLEWAX

Running down your face
Candlewax melted tears
You wipe them away
But they stick to your hand

Hurt is finding the truth in the blame
And
I am overflowing with acrid shame

Taking the trust that we had
And throwing it all away
I can see the opaque gauze fall
And your blue vision dims

Your smile unravels, love is packed
Away.
You are gone under a barrier of thickening wax

Sorry can't hold the heat to burn it away
So, I will pull down the sun and swallow it whole
Take you in my arms, try to re-ignite the love heat
As I beg a thousand pardons for my infidelity

THE TIMEGLASS

Silently and slowly the hands turn
Seconds rewind into the long ago
A sun rises in the East, a fiery glow
I can almost feel the heat of the burn
As the orbit stutters into opposite flow

I am counting the rotation roll
As spring falls into winter cold
Then autumn colours as leaves unfold
Going back, searching for a missing soul
It was lost long ago, a sad story to be told

Speeding through the lived-out days
Counting back to where you can be
Then finally the day comes into view
And my heart slows the reversing ways
Of Earths flow, and I finally see you

I step into the day, and it's clear
Like a picture, so perfectly matching memory
Tears blind me to your smile, so I don't see
You crossing the room, then arms hold me near
Finally, I have reached where I want to be

As I take the keys, that hold all of my fears
The time glass is silent, it waits patiently
For time to repair the change in history
No fateful trip now made, so no widow tears
Seconds click forward, into a new possibility

STARSTRUCK

I am a ghost in flight, across a starstruck sky

Taking a bite from the moon as I pass

Heading out into the forever ending

Of the universe, as it swirls with burning suns

Watch as I fly on borrowed wings

Feeling the love and joy fill my soul

And as I ignite into a dazzling light

The stars welcome me home

SUMMER FROST

How sharp the frost

That falls on the summer rose

As an unnatural winter

Covers a hot June land

And honey bees search for what is lost

In a place where nothing now grows

Tears fall as acid, for here we were.

A billion grains of sand.

NO MORE LOVE SONGS

Too bright is the sky
Golden blue the sparks fly
From a burning globe
And the seas bubble under its striking strobe

Smoke takes the last of breath
As water brings a cleansing death

Struck dumb the stars weep
Lost to an endless sleep
A world of enigmatic existence
How bright was its briefness?

ON THE OTHER SIDE

I am on the other side
Of the door
You are solid
As I am pale

Days, they no longer abide
Sleep, is no more
You sink in the flood
As I quietly sail

Farewell is a whisper
Seeping through the cracks
Bricks in the wall
I can't climb

Memory is what we were
A spark in the flashbacks
A fading footfall
It's my time, goodbye

WRECKED

I saw the clouds cry
Water fell like heavy heartbreak

I want to tell you a lie
I want to forgive and forsake
All that was between us

Too late, it's too late
You can't see me, I am faceless
I can yell, scream, berate

But you are boxed in silence
Deaf to my voice,
I scream into your silent absence

Wrecked, I wasn't given the choice
To be without you.

EYES CLOSED

Eyes closed
Breathing in air
Warmed by a dying sun
As life edges to the cliff
To a fall unbroken
Your secrets undisclosed
Now laid bare
Too late to be undone
You can say what if?
But no more lies to shun.

Breathe deep
Approach the end
Bring memories close
A light in the dark
Brings fond farewell
Drift into sleep
And slowly ascend
With calm repose
A quietened spark
In the stars now dwell

HELLO

You look, but don't hear
Each day the same
You speak my name

I am here

You look tired, and face worn
Eyes crusted from nights not rested
And days lived where strengths are tested

Listen

I need to say so much, or very little
So many minutes we had, lost in silence
Would trade my soul for one more sentence

My heart beats

Silently from the depths of my cold bed
But love, yes the love, that I forever gave
Beats a tune of the loudest drum from my grave

For you

I have lingered, but I can feel the pull
Gently leading me away, I can't fight, though I try
It's time. I leave you with love, but not goodbye

ALL I SEE

Hide the moon, I plead thee
Forever cover its neon glow
Pull out the stars, I beg
Let them shine eternity, no more

Let the Darkness reign
Let the world stop rotating
He is gone

Be still the bird's joyful song
Quiet the bees hum, the cats purr
Let the clocks lose their happy chime
And children's laughter fade to quiet

Let the silence fall
Let the night take away the sun
He is gone

He was the moon that filled my soul
His laughter, gave the world it's sound
His eyes, outshone the stars in the sky
His heart, showed a love, it was forever.

All I hear now is silence

All I see is falling rain

He is gone

Breathing is all that remains

WALKING THE WIRE

Balancing on a fragile wire
So high above me
Looking down on the pain
As I try to stop the fall
I know is coming
Tears, not mine, flood the plain

Focus, one step at a time
Sleep a forgotten language
As I walk in dreams
And figures in shaded form
Visit my days
Where nothing is at seems

Walking the tightrope
Silently amongst the loss
Breathing the air
Of a life planned absent
Of your voice
I can no longer share

I walk the wire
Waiting for the freefall

Into sedated black

So, I can dive into oceans

Of saline dreams

And bring you back

ENDINGS

Here we are

Ending

What is a new life

Beginning

To breathe in our

Birth

While we look for the

Dying

Of the life lived

Ending

LIFE AGAIN

Can sleep bring blindness?
And dreams block sound?
I no longer
See, submerged in nightmares

I haven't seen the sun today
Or heard the birds on the bough
I have been
Deaf, to voice and song

I thought I saw a spark
But it was brief in its illumination
A short-lived
Awakening, before sleep pulled me back

Here I can be lost, so I can be found
By you, who is gone from the world
I can still
Feel, the touch of your hand

You tether me to the living
Where voices sing and rainbows dazzle
I want to

Feel life again, without the pain

LIFETIME

Days spent counting the seconds

Grasping each moment

As years pass in a blink

Time to lament

As death opens the doorway

Lifetime lived

FEATHER FLIGHT

Capture the flight of feather flow
On lifting swells of waves, high and slow
Soar over an ocean of freckle dancing foam
Carried free, over land and sea, as I roam

Under cotton bleached clouds, moisture dry
The sun leads the way, across a lapis blue sky
Soaring on silent, soft feather flight
I glide through the hours, day into night

Watching as the planet turns below me
I can see electric lights spark up brightly
As cities become awake in the darkening gloom
Unaware of my continuing speeding zoom

I am caught up in an orbital ring
Kissing the moon as I pass, my wings sing
Lighting up stars against the universal black
I laugh, as I continue along the Angel track

DAYS OF SUMMER

Under a shadowed bower
Of olive-green scented leaves
I fall into morose reflection
As the heart grieves
For a love that was barely begun

For there was a time of you and me
In summer fields of broken hay
Where we spent our childhood years
Dancing amongst butterflies at play
And laughter came before the tears

How brief those hours in the sun
Before clouds gathered over the summer day
And a letter arrived at your door
I can still see the words pulling you away
A call for country, a call for war

I remember the day I said goodbye
There were no promises given
A brief hug, a touch of a hand
Then the train steamed out of the station
Taking you away to a distant land

For a year we kept in touch. Though
Letters were few and far between
And the last, how the ink was smeared
On paper that had once been clean
Filled with words strong and un-feared

Your body came home soon after
Your time with me frozen, as you were laid
To rest under branches of an old oak tree
I bring flowers each day, so the scent won't fade
A reminder of summer, and you and me

REMEMBER

In a land of silent birdsong
Where happiness dies
And the living shares the dead
With a community of flies
Where the explosions deafen the silence
And whispers of forgotten hope
Watch as fire welcomes the dawn
And float away like bubbles of soap
Too young to vote, but grown enough to die
Stand strong, stand true, their sergeant sings
So proud and brave they face the flurry
Of killing hornet stings
And as they charge across the killing field
They can't know at that dark time
How their sacrifice would change
All the lives, ever after, that's yours and mine

DUST

Silence blows across the arena
Killing the fire and destruction
Into an uneasy calm
And men rouse as if from sleep
And gaze with new born eyes
Across a land that is childless

Tears quench the hurt soul
As the dust of the dead
Are cast into a forgiving wind
And heart weary, they turn for home
Back to a life no longer familiar
And a world changed anew

The arena of battle left deserted
And a bird dares to break the silence
Singing with joyful song
As trees bud in promise and flowers
Bloom in a blaze of heart red
Covering the land, a healing balm

I THOUGHT I SAW

I thought I saw an Angel
As I stood knee deep in the mire
She was sat on the edge of hell
That burned, with a fiery, funeral pyre

Smiling, she looked down on me
With sadness in her eyes
As I sat and cleaned my rifle
Readying for the morning dies

Fifty men were with me yesterday
But only twenty now remain
Listening to the repeating booms
They huddle like children, against the explosive rain

Six hours to dawn, so the Sergeant says
Then over the top we are to rush
To charge into a field of craters
And fight through a thorny steel bush

For honour and for glory
Come the dawns shouting rally
For our home, for our family

So up we go into deaths valley

I think I see an Angel
Through the smoke and shrapnel stings
She is hovering above the stench
With outstretched golden wings

Come on lads, stay in line
Comes the Sergeants battle cry
We are nearly there just a few more steps
We can do it, we can try.

I see the smoke is clearing
There's a figure, his rifle raised high
His uniforms a different colour
But I see the same look in his eye

Our rifles are aimed, our triggers primed
But neither willing to take the shot
He looks just like my brother
He does, doesn't he? Maybe not.

Then his eyes they fill with wonder
And his rifle falls to the ground
He points over my shoulder
And lets out, a nervous sound.

And I know he has seen the Angel
So, I turn to take in the view
To find her standing in glory
Amongst the muddy, bloody goo

She smiles as the tears fall
And reaches out her hand
I know in that moment
Why she wanders the desolate land

I barely hear the noise behind me
As the gun is fired my way
Or feel the punch as something hits my chest
Making my body sway

Another soul for her collection
And as my body hits the ground
She reaches in and grabs a hold
In love and sadness my soul is bound

Too soon the guns are silent
There are no winners here today
A field of broken bodies
And the Angel goes on her way

Looking for the next battle

There is always one somewhere

Man fighting Man is as old as time

And the sorrow of this, the Angel will bear.

For all our souls.

BEST

My father was a soldier
He fought when he was young
Called up for honour, for duty
Was the nations song
At just sixteen he signed up
Leaving home and family
Heading to unknown lands
With thousands, he went happily

When I was ten I asked him
About the battles he had fought
About the medal he been given
And about the time he had been caught
He looked at me with distant eyes
And shook his head, just slight
Then in soft tone he said to me
Son I will tell, whether it's wrong or right

Many battles I was part
Of those horrors, I will not tell
I lost my friend. No enough,

I won't go into details of how he fell.
We fought, we died, we did our best.
The medal? It was for a life I could save
Through burning fields, I carried him
It was life or death, not brave.

Three years I spent in a war camp
Three years, until the war was done
In those years I saw torment and pain
He smiled grimly, man can be cruel, my son.
No, ask no more, past is past
There are things I don't want to re-see
I can only offer you one word of advice.
Live, and be the best of human you can be.

WESTERN WIND

Let me sail on a western wind
When my time on Earth is ended
Let me breathe the salted froth
As the path of my life is wended
No more scents of summer rose
Will I take into my breast
No more smell of Autumn leaves
When trees prepare for rest
I will no longer feel a summer rain
As it falls on flowered fields
I'll no longer hear the rumble of thunder
And the power that lightning wields
So, when all my life is done
Let me close my eyes and rest
Let me dream in loving slumber
As I sail warm seas, into the west.

TELLING TALES

I feel my history flow through me

Telling the tales of how my years played

Out, a theatre production of life. You see

I am the villain, the hero, the setting is staged

A plastic reproduction of where I performed

To an ever, changing crowd of folks

An audience of friendships lost and formed

Sometimes I've been the jester, they laughed at my jokes

Then drama, as my voice filled with emotion

I have danced for joy and danced for love

I have been the lover, and I have been a nun

I have been strong like a tiger, soft like a dove

Final act, and I can feel the spotlight glare

I feel the warmth of the audience glow

I can't see you, but I know you are there.

Thank you all for sharing, this wonderful show

AFTERWORD

Life in all of it's wondrous twists and turns life can bring joy and sorrow, in equal measure. Like night and day, each harmonise with each other. So that when grief and heartbreak plunge us into the dark. Be assured that there will be a sunrise and night will break into a new day.

You just need to wait for the sun to rise.

And it will.

ABOUT THE AUTHOR

Aj Harvey

Amanda lives in the UK with her husband Ian. When she is not locked away in her small office, typing away on her laptop, she is enjoying long walks in the North Yorkshrie countryside. As a child, she enjoyed the status of being a book-worm, spending her hours reading. Before finding her voice, writing poetry and short stories.